BILL MORGAN'S BEAT
AND OTHER SCENES
FOR COMMUNICATION

Robert Rainsbury

American Language Institute
New York University

Illustrated by Jeff Degnan

PRENTICE-HALL, INC.   Englewood Cliffs, New Jersey 07632

Library of Congress Cataloging-in-Publication Data

RAINSBURY, ROBERT, (date)
  Bill Morgan's beat and other scenes for communication.

  1. English language—Text-books for foreign speakers.
2. Communication.   I. Title.
PE1128.R24 1986   428.2'4   86-16869
ISBN   0-13-076282-2

Editorial and production supervision: Lisa A. Domínguez
Interior design: Lori Baronian
Cover design: Diane Saxe
Manufacturing buyer: Carol Bystrom

Printed in the United States of America
10 9 8 7 6 5 4 3 2 1

0-13-076282-2   01

Prentice-Hall International (UK) Limited, *London*
Prentice-Hall of Australia Pty. Limited, *Sydney*
Prentice-Hall Canada Inc., *Toronto*
Prentice-Hall Hispanoamericana, S.A., *Mexico*
Prentice-Hall of India Private Limited, *New Delhi*
Prentice-Hall of Japan, Inc., *Tokyo*
Prentice-Hall of Southeast Asia Pte. Ltd., *Singapore*
Editora Prentice-Hall do Brasil, Ltda., *Rio de Janeiro*

CONTENTS

INTRODUCTION

The aim of this book is to provide students with an opportunity to practice using language, both spoken and written, in a pleasant, unthreatening manner, employing words of their own choosing in an unstructured but nevertheless controlled situation. To this end, the book presents a series of stories that have been written in such a way that they can easily be turned into drama. Each story, that is, is written in clearly defined scenes.

The dialogue for the scenes is not given, and even indirect speech is avoided as far as possible. Also, the author has attempted to build the stories around situations and themes that reflect the students' own real-life situations and concerns. A number of the stories deal with persons recently arrived in an English-speaking country. Others call on the students to deal with value judgments of the kind they are required to make in their own lives. It is hoped that in performing these scenes, and taking part in the discussions that precede the performances, the students may find the opportunity to discuss their own problems in an easy, informal way. Finally, the students can practice their writing skills by writing the dialogue—by putting these little scenes into more permanent form. In this part of the lesson they are able, with the help of the teacher, to deal with matters of grammar and vocabulary that might be difficult to isolate in a fast-moving exchange of spoken language.

The method that will now be suggested for presenting these materials is the author's own. It is by no means the only possible method. Teachers who have taught this material experimentally have made it clear to the author that a number of variations can be employed successfully. These variants will also be discussed.

In the author's method, the teacher begins by presenting the story. This can be assigned in advance, or read silently in class, or the teacher and students can read it together, since the stories are all short. Then, after making sure that the story has been generally understood, the teacher has the students turn to the picture sequence, where they are given the opportunity to retell the story in their own words. This is intended to move them away from the language of the story and toward their own language, as well as to test comprehension. When the students have demonstrated that they can retell the story accurately, the teacher then passes to the discussion. Here the students explore the character and motivations of the people in the story, and discuss the issues and themes of the stories. Also, at this stage the students have the opportunity to relate the stories to their own experience. By taking full advantage of this part of the lesson, the teacher can make the dramatization fuller and more meaningful to the students than it might otherwise be. When this part of the lesson is concluded, the students should be ready to undertake the dramatization. The class chooses the actors. The drama is recreated in the classroom (in all the stories the settings have deliberately been kept simple) and the scenes are performed. After the performance, the teacher may elect to have further discussion. Perhaps the drama might be performed again, with different actors. After this, the teacher proceeds to the final phase, the writing. The students put on paper the dialogue they have been performing. This can be done individually or in groups (the author's preference). The teacher may elect to work with the groups, helping the students with the structure of the sentences and supplying needed vocabulary and idioms. This gives the teacher a good opportunity to deal with matters of register—helping students choose among several possible words or phrases the one that is appropriate for the given situation. After the completion of the writing, the students may wish to perform the dialogue again. If the writing was done by groups, each group might perform its version, with the class choosing the one they like best.

As stated above, teachers who have used this material have successfully employed several variations of the author's method. One teacher preferred to go from the discussion directly to the writing, and have the students perform the scene only after writing it. Another teacher omitted the writing phase altogether, which is certainly possible if the teacher wants to emphasize unstructured oral production rather than writing, with correct form as the primary goal. The materials allow for either option, or for an equal emphasis on both.

What is important is that the students' language in the lesson be their own and not something given by a textbook or a teacher. These materials deliberately avoid the notion of rigid control. There is a control, but it is imposed only by the logic of the story. The teacher works to refine and correct the raw material of the classroom, (or at least this teacher does), but even here the teacher is free to exercise a minimum of control or stay out of the proceedings altogether. The main point is that the students find the exercise a kind of game, but one that allows them to develop their skills and express feelings that are important to them.

I would like to express my indebtedness to those of my colleagues at the American Language Institute of New York University who read these lessons and offered their criticisms, especially to those who tried them in their classes. Specifically, I thank John Dumicich, Elaine Klein, Deborah Pires, Maxine Steinhaus, Carolyn Graham, Polly Davis, and, most particularly, Pat Duffy, whose careful reading and searching criticisms were of great value. Finally, and most importantly, I am deeply grateful to Carol, Salvador, Christina, George, Noriko, and the other members of my class who brought these scenes to life for the first time.

FIRST DAY
IN AMERICA

1

Rashid Mustafa recently came to the United States to study at an American university. On his first day after arriving at the university, he was assigned to a dormitory room. After unpacking his bag and putting his clothes away, he felt hungry, so he went to a little restaurant near the dormitory to get something to eat.

As he entered the restaurant and heard everyone around him speaking English, he began to feel very nervous. The waiter brought him a menu, but he couldn't remember the meaning of any of the words. When the waiter returned to take his order, Rashid couldn't speak to him. After a few minutes, the waiter understood the problem. He began to speak to Rashid in a kindly way. He himself had come from Greece thirty years before, and at that time he had had trouble with the language. He understood how Rashid was feeling. He explained all this. Then he took the menu. Slowly he explained what some of the words meant. Rashid's English began to come back to him, and after a few minutes he was able to order a roast beef sandwich and coffee. The waiter was so pleasant and helpful that Rashid thanked him and left him a good tip. And he went back to that restaurant for lunch every day.

I. Using the following pictures, tell the story you have just read in your own words.

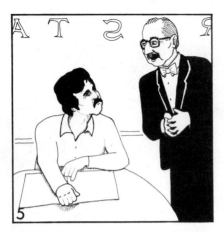

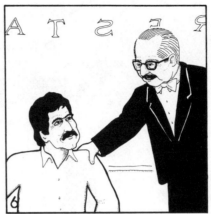

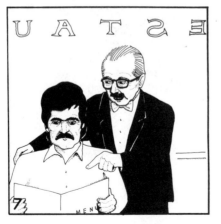

QUESTIONS FOR DISCUSSION

1. What words would you use to describe Rashid in the restaurant? The waiter?

2. How do you call a waiter? How should you behave toward a waiter? How should a waiter behave toward a customer?

3. Have you had an experience like Rashid's? Can you tell the class about it?

II. Act out the story you have just read and heard. Choose students to take the parts of the persons in the story and improvise the dialogue. There is one scene and two characters.

Setting: The Restaurant
Characters: Rashid
                    The Waiter

III. Write the dialogue for the scene you have just acted out.

NAME OF RESTAURANT	TYPE OF RESTAURANT	PRICE RANGE	TYPICAL MENU ITEMS	HOURS OPEN	BREAKFAST?	TABLE SERVICE?	COUNTER SERVICE?

1. Investigation

a. Talk with other students in your class, or other international students, or persons in your community who come from other countries. Find out what their first day in this country was like. Are there problems everybody encounters? Could something be done to make the experience easier? Prepare a report and present it to your class.

b. Find out what kinds of eating places are available in your neighborhood and, using the information you have gotten, fill out the chart that follows. Prepare a report for your class and distribute the chart.

2. Quick Sketch

Improvise a scene between a person who has just arrived in an English-speaking country and a clerk in a drugstore or department store.

2

A COMPLAINT

Mrs. Gómez went to Fleagle's Department Store and bought an electric alarm clock. When she got home, she discovered that it didn't work, so she decided to return it to the store. At the store she spoke to a sales clerk, who sent her to the complaint department on the seventh floor. When she got there, she tried to explain her problem to the clerk. He had trouble understanding her and became very impatient. He asked her for her receipt. She looked all through her purse but couldn't find it. The clerk became even more impatient. He suggested that she had bought the clock in another store. He didn't remember seeing that brand of clock in Fleagle's. Mrs. Gómez was almost ready to cry. The clerk said he couldn't take any more time to talk to her. Just then Mrs. Gómez found the sales slip. The clerk became pleasant. He apologized to her. He offered her the choice of a refund or another clock. Mrs. Gómez decided to take the clock, and went home happily.

I. Using the following pictures, tell the story you have just read in your own words.

QUESTIONS FOR DISCUSSION

1. What words would you use to describe Mrs. Gómez in the complaint department? The clerk she spoke to?

2. How should a store clerk act toward a customer? A customer toward a clerk?

3. Have you ever had an unpleasant experience like the one in the story? Can you tell the class about it?

II. Act out the story you have just read and heard. Choose students to take the parts of the persons in the story and improvise the dialogue. There are two scenes and three characters.

Scene 1   Setting: Counter at Fleagle's Department Store
           Characters: Mrs. Gómez
                      A Sales Clerk

Scene 2   Setting: The Complaint Department at Fleagle's
           Characters: Mrs. Gómez
                      A Clerk

III. Write the dialogue for the scenes you have just acted out.

EXTRA ACTIVITIES _____

1. Investigation

Find out the refund and exchange policies of several department stores or other large stores in the community where you are studying. Are there city or state laws that apply to returning articles to stores? Prepare a report for the class from your information.

2. Quick Sketch

Improvise a dialogue between a person who wants to exchange an article of clothing he or she received as a gift and a clerk in the exchange department of the store where the article was purchased.

A MUGGING

3

One night Sally Harris was walking home from work when a man approached her and stood in front of her. He had a gun in his hand. He demanded her purse. She gave it to him, and he ran away down the street.

When she got home, she was shaking so badly she could hardly take off her coat. Her roommate, Jane, wanted to know what had happened, but Sally was still so frightened that she could not speak for a minute. When she finally told Jane what had happened, Jane wanted Sally to go to the police station immediately. Sally was afraid to go, but Jane insisted and promised to go with her.

At the police station a detective asked Sally many questions. He wanted a description of the man, and he wanted to know exactly what the man had said and done. When she finished, the detective excused himself and left the room. When he returned, he was holding Sally's purse in his hand. The robber had run right into the arms of a policeman. Sally and Jane thanked everyone and went home.

I. Using the following pictures, tell the story you have just read in your own words.

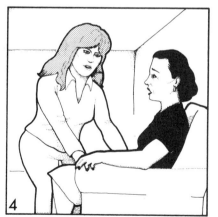

16

QUESTIONS FOR DISCUSSION

1. What words would you use to describe Sally after the mugging? Jane? The detective?
2. What should an individual do if he finds himself in a similar situation? Should he cooperate with the robber? Should he be afraid to go to the police?
3. Have you had an experience like the one in the story? Can you tell the class about it?

II. Act out the story you have just read and heard. Choose students to take the parts of the persons in the story, and improvise the dialogue. There are three scenes and four characters.

Scene 1	Setting:	The Street
	Characters:	Sally
		The Mugger
Scene 2	Setting:	Sally's Apartment
	Characters:	Sally
		Jane
Scene 3	Setting:	The Police Station
	Characters:	Sally
		Jane
		The Detective

III. Write the dialogue for the scenes you have just acted out.

EXTRA ACTIVITIES _____

1. Investigation

Talk to the appropriate people in the community where you are studying and prepare a report on the following:

a. How do you report a crime to the police?

b. What should you do in case you are a victim? How can you protect yourself? What do the police recommend doing and not doing?

2. Quick Sketch

Improvise a dialogue between a policeman and a person who has just returned home to find his or her apartment has been robbed. The scene is the apartment.

FREDDY, THE CLASS CLOWN

4

Freddy Potts is a student in an American high school. He is the class clown, always thinking of something to say or do that will make the other students laugh. One day while the class was waiting for the teacher to arrive, Freddy drew a caricature of the teacher on the blackboard. Everybody laughed, and they all thought, Freddy included, that the teacher would also laugh when he saw it. But when the teacher arrived, he became furious and demanded to know who had drawn the caricature. The other students glanced at Freddy, but he sat in his seat and said nothing.

The teacher then went to Mr. Johnson, the principal, and demanded that he do something. Mr. Johnson was a kind man. He tried to tell the teacher that whoever had done the drawing had meant no harm, but the teacher remained angry. He wanted the student to be punished. Mr. Johnson agreed to call in the students one by one and question them.

Meanwhile, in the classroom, the other students spoke with Freddy. They told him that if he confessed, he would probably not be punished severely. They knew Mr. Johnson was kind. But Freddy was not convinced. He was often in trouble because of his pranks and his parents were already angry at him. The students told him that they would not inform on him, but Freddy could see that they did not like to be in this position. Then a messenger arrived from the principal's office. Mr. Johnson wanted to see Mike Wilson. Mike was Freddy's best friend.

In the principal's office, Mike tried to evade Mr. Johnson's questions. He didn't want to lie, but he didn't want to name his friend either. So he answered every question with another question, or with a vague answer. But in the middle of the questioning, Freddy walked in. He confessed everything and said he had meant no harm. Mr. Johnson scolded him severely, then he suggested that Freddy apologize to the teacher. When the teacher saw that Freddy was genuinely sorry, he accepted his apology and shook hands with him. The principal warned Freddy not to do it again, and the incident ended happily.

I. Using the following pictures, tell the story you have just read in your own words.

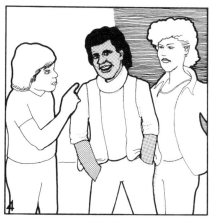

QUESTIONS FOR DISCUSSION

1. Was the teacher right to get angry about the drawing?

2. What words would you use to describe Freddy? The principal, Mr. Johnson? The teacher?

3. Have you ever had a friend like Freddy? Can you tell the class about him or her?

4. Do you think Freddy was wrong to keep quiet? If you were a student in that class, would you promise not to inform? Or would you tell the principal who the guilty person was?

5. Have you ever done something or said something that was supposed to be funny, but instead made someone angry? Can you tell the class about it?

II. Act out the story you have just read and heard. Choose students to take the parts of the persons in the story and improvise the dialogue. There are four scenes and five characters. The rest of the class can take the parts of the students in the class.

Scene 1 Setting: The Classroom
         Characters: Freddy
                       The Students
                       The Teacher
Scene 2 Setting: The Principal's Office
         Characters: The Teacher
                       The Principal

Scene 3 Setting: The Classroom
Characters: Freddy
The Students
A Messenger

Scene 4 Setting: The Principal's Office
Characters: Mike
The Teacher
The Principal
Freddy

III. Write the dialogue for the scenes you have just acted out.

1. Debate

Choose two students or two teams to debate the following questions:

    a. Is it wrong to inform on another person when you know he or she has done something wrong?

    b. Does it make a difference if the guilty person is a friend?

2. Quick Sketch

A student has been accused of stealing something. Everyone in the class knows he is innocent and also who the real thief is. Improvise a dialogue between two students—one who thinks the class should inform on the real thief and one who thinks informing is always wrong.

5

LAID OFF

Jim Schneider works as a foreman in an auto assembly plant. He has a wife and an eight-year-old daughter. They live in a house in the suburbs and, until now, have gotten along very well on Jim's salary. But one day Jim's boss sent for him. Jim went to his office and his boss asked him to sit down. The boss started talking about business conditions in the auto industry. Then he discussed conditions in this plant. The company was losing money and it would be necessary to take steps to reduce expenses. The boss told Jim the company was going to lay off a number of workers, and Jim was among them. He would, of course, receive two weeks' pay, and as soon as the company's financial situation improved, the company would be glad to have Jim back again.

Jim ate lunch with Jerry Fields, another foreman who had been given the same news. At first they were angry. They spoke bitterly about the company they had worked hard for and that was now abandoning them. But then they became calmer. They discussed other possibilities for work. They tried to think of other companies that might need men in this city or cities nearby. They tried to think of other kinds of work they could do. They tried to cheer each other up, but they did not feel very hopeful.

At home that night, Jim broke the news to his wife. They immediately started to make plans. They looked at their bank book, and added in the two weeks' pay Jim would be receiving from the company. They looked at their budget, and went over their expenses and future plans. They had planned to buy certain things, but now some of those things would have to wait. Other things—medical and dental expenses, for example—would have to be paid somehow. The Schneiders had planned a family vacation for the summer. They would have to give that up. Then Jim's wife made a proposal. She had been a secretary before her marriage, and she was a good one. She thought she could find work again. Jim didn't like this, but he agreed. He also agreed to stay home and do the shopping and housekeeping, and get their daughter's breakfast and lunch for her, although he liked that even less. After the Schneiders finished their discussion, they felt a little better. They would probably be all right for the immediate future. But there would be difficult times ahead if Jim didn't get a job soon.

I. Using the following pictures, tell the story you have just read in your own words.

29

1. What words would you use to describe Jim Schneider? His wife? His boss?

2. Are Jim and Jerry right to be angry at the company? Is the company at fault?

3. Is Jim right to agree to his wife's working? Is he right to agree to do the housework and take care of his daughter? If you found yourself in a similar situation, would you agree to these things?

II. Act out the story you have just read and heard. Choose students to take the parts of the persons in the story, and improvise the dialogue. There are three scenes and four characters.

Scene 1	Setting:	The Boss' Office
	Characters:	Jim
		His Boss
Scene 2	Setting:	The Company Lunchroom
	Characters:	Jim
		Jerry Fields
Scene 3	Setting:	Jim's Home
	Characters:	Jim
		Jim's Wife

III. Write the dialogue for the scenes you have just acted out.

1. Investigation

Talk to the appropriate people in the community where you are studying and prepare a report on the following:

a. Is unemployment a serious problem in this community? Is there a group or several groups of people who are particularly affected?

b. What assistance do the city and state provide for an unemployed worker? If the worker belongs to a union, what kind of help is available to him?

2. Quick Sketch

Improvise a dialogue between the following two persons:

a. Two laid-off workers who meet at the unemployment office.

b. A laid-off worker and his eight-year-old child, in which the father attempts to explain why he isn't working.

6 MAKING A FILM

Marcia Cooper is taking a course in filmmaking. She is making a short film as part of her course requirements. Last Saturday she took her equipment and several student actors to a park to film a scene. Things did not turn out the way Marcia had planned, however.

The scene she was filming concerned a boy and girl who were separating. They were supposed to talk together, and the boy was supposed to tell the girl that he was leaving her for another girl. The girl was supposed to cry while the boy remained indifferent. Marcia set up her camera, placed the actors on a park bench, and called "Action."

The actors played their scene very convincingly. The girl begged the boy not to leave her, and the boy told her to be quiet and stop crying. Soon other people in the park began to notice the scene. Unfortunately, they didn't notice the camera, which was some distance away. An old lady who was walking through the park stopped to listen. She got very angry at the way the boy was behaving. She walked into the scene and started scolding the boy. He tried to explain, but she wouldn't listen.

She finally got so angry that she hit him on the head with her umbrella. When Marcia's assistant came over to her and tried to explain they were making a film, she hit *her*. By this time a small crowd had gathered, and people were taking sides with either the boy or the girl. Things got so bad that a policeman came and said he would arrest everybody if they didn't calm down. Then somebody noticed Marcia's camera and realized that this was all a film. When the crowd realized it, they all started laughing. Even the policeman had to laugh. As for Marcia, she kept filming. She had decided to change her film from a serious story to a comedy.

I. Using the following pictures, tell the story you have just read in your own words.

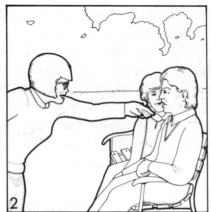

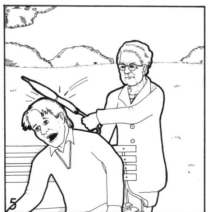

34

35

QUESTIONS FOR DISCUSSION

1. What words would you use to describe Marcia? The old lady?

2. Have you ever been embarrassed because you misunderstood something that was happening? Can you tell the class about it?

3. Have you ever seen a movie being made? Can you tell the class about it?

II. Act out the story you have just read and heard. Choose students to take the parts of the persons in the story, and improvise the dialogue. There is one scene and there are six principal characters. There are a number of extra parts that can be taken by the rest of the class.

Setting: A Park
Characters: Marcia
             Her Assistant
             An Actor
             An Actress
             An Old Lady
             A Policeman
             A Crowd of People

III. Write the dialogue for the scene you have just acted out.

1. Debate

Many people feel that movies are a bad influence on the people who watch them because they give a false picture of life and they often make bad things like crime and violence seem attractive. Others feel that movies are a help in learning about life. Some even say that the movies are an art form, part of the literature of our time. Choose two students or two teams to debate the question:

Are movies a good or bad influence on our lives?

2. Quick Sketch

The author of the screenplay that Marcia was filming was very upset when he learned that Marcia was changing it from a serious story to a comedy. Marcia spoke with him and tried to convince him that it was a better story done this way. Improvise a scene with these two characters.

7 CAB DRIVER

Young Soon Park came to this country from Korea with his family five years ago. Now he is attending a university. At night and on weekends he helps with the family expenses by driving a cab. Last Saturday he had a typical day.

First, he picked up a well-dressed man who wanted to go to the airport. The man noticed Young Soon Park's accent and asked him where he was from. Then he asked him a lot of questions about his country, its government, and the daily life of its people. He also wanted to know about Young Soon. When he found out he was a student, the man made a big speech about America being the land of opportunity and about the value of hard work. When he got to the airport, he told Young Soon to keep at it and gave him a good tip.

At the airport Young Soon picked up a girl. She told him she had come to the city because she wanted to be an actress. She planned to study acting and also to try and get parts in plays. Young Soon told her about a hotel he knew where the rates were low and the neighborhood was safe. He also recommended a good restaurant near the hotel that served good food at reasonable prices. He gave her some other good suggestions about how to live cheaply in the city. She decided to try the hotel, so Young Soon took her there. Because he knew she was going to need her money, he refused a tip.

Next he picked up an older woman who was going uptown to visit her son. She criticized his driving constantly, telling him he was going too fast and taking the wrong streets. She accused him of going out of the way in order to increase the fare. Young Soon was angry because none of these things were true, but he kept quiet. When they got to her destination, she gave him a ten-cent tip. This made him really angry, but he merely thanked her.

By then, it was time for his morning coffee break. He went to a coffee shop where many cab drivers went. He saw another cab driver he knew, and sat down with him. He started to tell the man about his last passenger. As he told the story, the other man started laughing. At first Young Soon was angry at the man, but then he began to see the humor in it, and he began laughing with him.

I. Using the following pictures, tell the story you have just read in your own words.

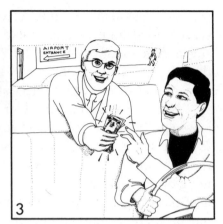

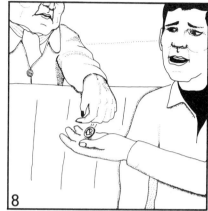

┌─ *QUESTIONS FOR DISCUSSION* ─────────────────────┐

1. What words would you use to describe Young Soon? The well-dressed man? The young girl? The lady?

2. What is the proper tip for a cab driver? What other persons do you tip, and how much?

3. What kind of experiences (good or bad) have you had with cab drivers?

II. Act out the story you have just read and heard. Choose students to take the parts of the persons in the story, and improvise the dialogue. There are four scenes and five characters.

Scene 1	Setting:	Inside the Cab
	Characters:	Young Soon Park
		A Well-Dressed Man
Scene 2	Setting:	Inside the Cab
	Characters:	Young Soon Park
		A Young Girl
Scene 3	Setting:	Inside the Cab
	Characters:	Young Soon Park
		An Older Woman
Scene 4	Setting:	A Coffee Shop
	Characters:	Young Soon Park
		Another Cab Driver

III. Write the dialogue for the scenes you have just acted out.

1. Investigation

Talk to the appropriate people in the community where you are studying and prepare a report on the following:

    a. What are the typical problems a cab driver has with passengers?

    b. What do people who frequently take cabs complain about in cab drivers?

2. Quick Sketch

Improvise a dialogue between a cab driver and a difficult passenger. Suggestion: A passenger who is drunk, bossy, new in town, or not fluent in English.

8 *BILL MORGAN'S BEAT*

Bill Morgan is a policeman. He walks a beat in an uptown neighborhood where he has worked for twenty years. They don't always like policemen uptown, but they like Bill because they know he likes them. One day recently, Bill was walking along Monroe Avenue, which is a small shopping area. He stopped first at a gas station, where he talked with the owner about his business. The owner told Bill about the rising prices and the difficulty of finding a good mechanic. He also spoke about the increase in gas station robberies. He hadn't been robbed yet, but it was on his mind.

Then Bill stopped at a newsstand to talk to the dealer. Bill knew the man's wife was in the hospital where she had just had a baby girl. He congratulated the man and asked about his wife's health. The dealer offered Bill a cigar, but Bill doesn't smoke.

By this time, Bill was getting thirsty, so he decided to stop in López' grocery store and get a Coke. He always enjoyed stopping to have a chat with Mr. and Mrs. López. As he walked in the door, he saw several neighborhood people whom he recognized and a stranger. Mrs. López was behind the counter, but instead of smiling and talking as usual, she seemed nervous. Bill's instinct told him that something was wrong. He got his Coke, paid for it, and, as he turned to leave, his eye fell on the stranger. Bill noticed the man had his hand in his pocket. Bill realized he had interrupted a robbery. He kept walking as if he hadn't noticed anything, then suddenly he turned, drew his gun, and put it against the stranger's back. He ordered him to take his hand out of his pocket slowly, and, as he had suspected, the man was holding a gun. Bill quickly ordered him to drop it, and put the man in handcuffs. When the man was safely in handcuffs, he called for a squad car. All the people in the store crowded around Bill to thank him for what he had done.

I. Using the following pictures, tell the story you have just read in your own words.

46

QUESTIONS FOR DISCUSSION

1. What words would you use to describe Bill Morgan?
2. The story says "they don't always like policemen uptown." Why do you think that is?
3. What kind of experiences (good or bad) have you had with policemen?

II. Act out the story you have just read and heard. Choose students to take the parts of the persons in the story and improvise the dialogue. There are three scenes and five characters. In the last scene there are two or three extra parts.

Scene 1	Setting:	A Gas Station
	Characters:	Bill Morgan
		The Station Owner
Scene 2	Setting:	A Newsstand
	Characters:	Bill Morgan
		The Newsdealer
Scene 3	Setting:	The López Grocery Store
	Characters:	Bill Morgan
		Mrs. López
		A Robber
		Several Customers

III. Write the dialogue for the scenes you have just acted out.

EXTRA ACTIVITIES

1. Investigation

How do people in your neighborhood feel about the police? Do they feel adequately protected? Do the police use foot patrols or police cars? Which do the neighborhood people prefer? What other protection would they like to see, and in what areas do they think they need protection? Talk to some neighborhood people—residents and businessmen—and find out what they think. Make a report to the class.

2. Debate

In England, the police are not permitted to carry guns. Some people feel that there are too many people carrying guns in this country. Others think that gun control laws in some states are too strict and do not permit private citizens to protect themselves. Find out about the laws in the community where you are living, and choose two students or two teams to debate the question:

> Are gun control laws too strict, not strict enough, or adequate as they are?

9 *A YOUNG SHOPLIFTER*

One day a clerk in a bookstore saw a young boy slip a paperback book into his pocket. When the boy tried to leave the store, the clerk blocked his way. The proprietor of the store took the book out of the boy's pocket and told the clerk to call the police. They arrived a few minutes later and arrested the boy.

At the police station the boy, his parents, the police officers, and the bookstore proprietor all met together. The boy's parents offered to pay for the book, but the store owner would not accept the money because the boy's parents wanted him to drop charges against their son. The store owner told the parents how much money he lost every week because of shoplifters. He decided he had to start getting tough. He also thought that young men whose parents pay for their crimes go out and steal again with no fear. He thought this had to be stopped. The police booked the boy and released him in the custody of his parents.

Back home, the boy had an argument with his parents. He explained that he saw a book he wanted, but he didn't have enough money to buy it so he took it. It was the easiest thing to do. He had done it before without being caught. A paperback book doesn't cost a lot of money, so he was sure the store owner wouldn't suffer that much of a loss. Besides, he knew that many store owners overcharge their customers. He had also seen shopkeepers deliberately short-change their customers. He knew a group of men who paid a policeman every week so they could park in a convenient but illegal spot. He reminded his father that he had admitted not telling the whole truth when he paid his income tax. All adults cheat, the boy said. It was hypocritical for them to lecture young people. The boy's parents tried to answer his arguments as he made each point, but they got nowhere. Finally, the boy walked out of the room. He felt there was no point in going on with the discussion. The parents were deeply troubled. They asked each other how they could convince a young person to be honest in a world with so much dishonesty in it.

I. Using the following pictures, tell the story you have just read in your own words.

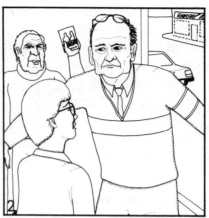

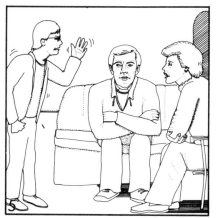

QUESTIONS FOR DISCUSSION

1. Was the store owner right in having the boy arrested?

2. With whom do you sympathize more, the boy or his parents?

3. Do you think everybody cheats, as the boy claimed?

4. How would you answer the question that ends the story?

II. Act out the story you have just read and heard. Choose students to take the parts of the persons in the story, and improvise the dialogue. There are three scenes and seven characters.

Scene 1 Setting: A Bookstore
          Characters: A Young Boy
                       A Clerk
                       The Store Owner

Scene 2 Setting: A Police Station
          Characters: Two Police Officers
                       The Boy
                       The Store Owner
                       The Boy's Parents

Scene 3 Setting: The Boy's Home
          Characters: The Boy
                       His Parents

III. Write the dialogue for the scenes you have just acted out.

1. Investigation

Talk to several store owners in the community where you are studying and find out the answers to the following questions:

    a. How much of a problem is shoplifting for them?

    b. How do the store owners guard against shoplifting?

    c. What do the store owners do when they catch a shoplifter?

Prepare a report for the class from your information.

2. Debate

Choose two students or two teams to debate the following questions:

    a. Is shoplifting a serious crime and should it carry a severe penalty?

    b. Is shoplifting ever justified?

3. Quick Sketch

A boy offers a book to a girl as a gift. She knows he has taken it without paying for it, and doesn't want to accept it. She likes the boy in many ways, but is disturbed by his shoplifting habits. Improvise a scene with these two characters.

10 THREE DREAMS I
HILDA'S DREAM

Hilda and Hector have been married for twenty years. They love each other, but each has habits the other would like to change.

Hector smokes cigars and their thick smoke sometimes fills the room. Hilda hates the smell. In the evening, he likes to sit in front of the TV and drink beer. Sometimes he falls asleep and snores. He loves to watch football games on TV. Hilda doesn't understand football and it bores her. And Hector never picks up his clothes. He leaves them all over the house and won't help with the housework. One night Hilda had a dream.

She dreamed she came into the house and everything was sparkling clean. Hector came out of the kitchen with a broom in his hand. He had decided to do the housecleaning. He took her into the bedroom. All his clothes were neatly put away. Since the house was clean, she could sit down for once and watch TV. Hector wanted to know what program she wanted to see. He had decided to give up football because he noticed she didn't enjoy it. He had also decided to give up beer and cigars. The beer made him too sleepy, and smoking was probably bad for his health. He sat down beside her and took her hand, which he had not done for years. But suddenly Hilda heard a strange noise and she woke up. Hector was snoring again.

I. Using the following pictures, tell the story you have just read in your own words.

58

59

60

━ *QUESTIONS FOR DISCUSSION* ━━━━━━━━━━━━━━

1. What words would you use to describe Hector?
2. Do you know a couple like Hector and Hilda? Can you tell the class about them?

II. Act out the story you have just read and heard. Choose students to take the parts of the persons in the story and improvise the dialogue. There is one scene and there are two characters.

Setting: Hector and Hilda's Living Room
Characters: Hector
                    Hilda

III. Write the dialogue for the scene you have just acted out.

1. Debate

Does a wife have the right to expect her husband to share in the housework—cleaning, washing dishes, cooking, and so on? Choose two students or two teams to debate this subject.

2. Quick Sketch

Hilda has a next-door neighbor who sometimes drops by in the morning for coffee. Sometimes Hilda discusses her feelings toward Hector and her problems with him. What do the two women say to each other? Improvise a scene with the two women.

11 *THREE DREAMS* II
HECTOR'S DREAM

Hector loves Hilda, but he would like to see some changes, too. When he gets home at night, he's tired. He likes to relax with a good cigar and a beer. But Hilda always nags him about these things. Sometimes he's so tired after working all day that he falls asleep. But instead of being sympathetic, Hilda gets angry because he snores. His favorite sport in the world is football, but when he sits down to watch it on TV, Hilda makes sarcastic remarks about what a boring game it is. Hector wishes she would try harder to understand him. The same night Hilda had her dream, Hector also had a dream.

He dreamed he came home as usual, but this time Hilda met him at the door with a big smile. She led him to his favorite chair and asked him if he would like a beer. She went out to the kitchen and returned with a bottle of beer and a glass on a tray. And beside them was a beautiful big cigar! After he poured the beer, she asked to taste it. She smiled with surprise. She liked it! Hector turned on the TV. There was a wonderful football game on. Hilda sat down to watch it with him, and asked him to explain the game to her so they could enjoy it together.

But suddenly Hector felt someone shaking him by the shoulder. He woke up. Hilda was looking at him angrily, and he knew he had been snoring again.

I. Using the following pictures, tell the story you have just read in your own words.

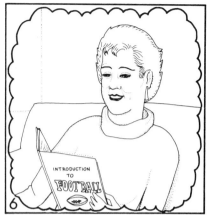

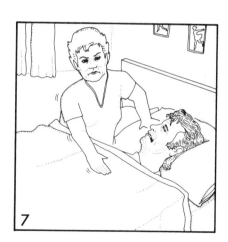

65

II. Act out the story you have just read and heard. Choose students to take the parts of the persons in the story and improvise the dialogue. There is one scene and there are two characters.

Setting: Hector and Hilda's Living Room
Characters: Hector
                Hilda

III. Write the dialogue for the scene you have just acted out.

Quick Sketches

a. Hector has a good friend whom he has known for years. Sometimes he tells his friend about his feelings toward Hilda and his problems with her. What do the two men say to each other? Improvise a scene with these two characters.

b. Hector and Hilda have finally agreed to see a marriage counselor. How do they defend themselves and present their sides of the question? What advice do they receive? Improvise a scene with the two of them and the marriage counselor.

12   *THREE DREAMS   III*
HAROLD'S DREAM

Harold Brewster works in an office. He has worked there since he finished high school. His boss is a big man with a loud voice who likes to shout at everybody. Harold has a secretary who is young and pretty. Harold has the feeling that she laughs at him behind his back because he's getting older and fatter and losing his hair. One night, after working late on a special report, Harold got home very tired. He went to bed early, and he had a strange dream.

He dreamed he was arriving at his office. As he walked in the door, his secretary looked at him and pointed her finger and started laughing. He had forgotten his tie. Then his boss walked in and started shouting that Harold had forgotten to shave. He tried to apologize to both people, but they paid no attention and went on laughing and shouting. Then the boss said he wanted to see Harold's report right away. Harold went to his desk. The report wasn't there. Then he noticed the cleaning woman leaving the office. His secretary said that she had taken the report and put it in with the trash. Harold called to the cleaning woman, but she kept on going and left the office. Harold's boss came out again and demanded the report. When Harold told him what had happened, the boss fired him. Then, suddenly, Harold felt angry. He started shouting back at the boss. He told him what he thought of him and of the way he treated his employees. He said all of the things he had wanted to say for years. The boss ran out of the room, but Harold followed him. When he had finished saying all he wanted to say, he turned around. His secretary was looking at him adoringly. She told him what a wonderful man he was, and she took his hand. At that point Harold woke up. It was another working day, and it was raining.

I. Using the following pictures, tell the story you have just read in your own words.

┌─── *QUESTIONS FOR DISCUSSION* ─────────────┐

  1. What words would you use to describe Harold? His secretary? His boss?

  2. Do you think Harold will ever talk to his boss in real life as he does in the dream?

  3. Do you know someone like Harold? Can you tell the class about him?

└──┘

II. Act out the story you have just read and heard. Choose students to take the parts of the persons in the story and improvise the dialogue. There is one scene and three characters.

    Setting: Harold's Office
    Characters: Harold
                  The Boss
                  Harold's Secretary

III. Write the dialogue for the scene you have just acted out.

1. Investigation

How do other people feel about dreams? Do they reveal the dreamer's feelings? Do they foretell the future? Are they completely meaningless and unimportant? Ask a number of people in your class, your school, or your community and prepare a report for your class.

2. Quick Sketches

a. Find someone in the class who has had an interesting dream—funny, frightening, whatever—and act it out.

b. Harold goes to see a psychiatrist every week. On one of his visits he described his dream to the doctor. What do you think the psychiatrist told him? What advice did he give him? Improvise the scene between Harold and the psychiatrist.

13 *CARLOS AND ELINOR* I

Carlos Vega is studying English at an American university. His roommate is an American named Dave Norman. They are good friends. One day Dave told Carlos about a dance that was being given by the university to celebrate the coming spring break. Carlos had heard about the dance, but he didn't want to go because he didn't know any American girls and he felt embarrassed when he tried speaking English to anyone but Dave. But Dave wanted him to go. He thought that Carlos could practice his English at the dance and that it would be good for him to meet some American girls. After some discussion, Carlos agreed to go. He felt nervous when he thought about it, but he felt excited, too. He loved to dance.

When they arrived at the dance, the dance floor was crowded, and all the people seemed to know each other. Carlos felt very shy. A minute later he saw a girl standing by herself. Then Dave saw her too. He knew her, and brought Carlos over and introduced him. The girl's name was Elinor. She and Carlos started talking and they very soon discovered

that they had interests in common. Elinor had studied Spanish and
could speak a little. After only a short time, Carlos felt that he had
made a friend. He asked Elinor to dance, and they went onto the dance
floor together.

I. Using the following pictures, tell the story you have just read in
your own words.

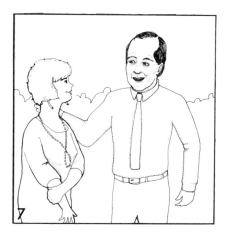

┌─ *QUESTIONS FOR DISCUSSION* ─────────────────┐

1. What kind of person is Carlos? What words would you use to describe him? How would you describe Dave?

2. What can a young person like Carlos or Elinor do to meet a person of the opposite sex? Is the answer different for boys and girls? Why?

3. What words or expressions does a boy use to ask a girl to dance? How does she reply?

4. How do you feel about speaking English with strangers? How did you feel when you first started to learn the language?

└──┘

II. Act out the story you have just read and heard. Choose students to take the parts of the persons in the story and improvise the dialogue. There are two scenes and three characters.

Scene 1 Setting: Carlos' room
         Characters: Carlos
                        Dave
Scene 2 Setting: The Dance
         Characters: Carlos
                        Dave
                        Elinor

III. Write the dialogue for the scenes you have just acted out.

1. Investigation

Do young men and women in your school find it easy to meet? To what kinds of places do they go for this purpose? Are there places where women cannot go without an escort? Do a study and report to the class.

2. Quick Sketch

After Elinor got home from the dance, she told her roommate about the boy she had met. What did she say? How did her roommate react? Improvise a scene between these two people.

14 *CARLOS AND ELINOR* II

After that first night, Carlos and Elinor continued to see each other. They dated every weekend, and soon people got used to seeing them together everywhere. When the school year ended, they both went home to spend the summer with their families.

Soon Elinor was seeing her old friends and going places with them again. But she thought about Carlos and wrote to him every week. She got letters back from him.

One evening Elinor and her mother had a talk. Her mother had noticed the letters from Carlos. She had also noticed how often Elinor spoke about him. She wanted to talk to Elinor about it, to find out how serious things were, but she didn't want to appear to be interfering in her daughter's life. So she spoke, not about Carlos and Elinor, but about herself. She had met Elinor's father when she herself was a college student. It was love at first sight, and they had married after a very short engagement. She had left college, and soon found herself with a household to manage, and later a child. She had never returned to school.

Her marriage was a happy one, and she had never regretted marrying her husband, but she did regret never finishing college. And when she thought about how little she had known about Elinor's father when she married him, she realized it was very fortunate that things had turned out as well as they had. She could easily have made a big mistake. Elinor understood why her mother was telling her these things, but she didn't let her mother know that she did. Later that night, as she was writing a letter to Carlos, she stopped and thought for a long time about her mother's words. But she went back to the letter and finished it.

I. Using the following pictures, tell the story you have just read in your own words.

QUESTIONS FOR DISCUSSION

1. What words would you use to describe Elinor? Her mother?
2. Do you think her mother was right to speak to Elinor as she did?
3. What do you think about early marriages—are they a good idea or not?
4. In some parts of the world, parents arrange marriages for their children. Do you think this is a good idea? Would it solve the problem of early marriages that don't turn out well?

II. Act out the story you have just read and heard. Choose students to take the parts of the persons in the story and improvise the dialogue. There is one scene and two characters.

Setting: The living room of Elinor's house
Characters: Elinor
  Her Mother

III. Write the dialogue for the scene you have just acted out.

EXTRA ACTIVITIES —————————————————

Quick Sketch

After she had the talk with Elinor, Elinor's mother discussed the conversation with her husband. What did Elinor's parents say to each other? Improvise a scene between these two persons.

CARLOS AND ELINOR   III

Carlos enjoyed his summer, too. It felt good to see his parents and friends and to speak his native language again. It was good to be home.

One evening he and his father had a talk. His father had made the decision to send him to school in America, and he didn't regret it, but he was beginning to worry. He was afraid that Carlos would become too American, that he might meet an American girl and marry her and stay in America, and have children who would grow up speaking only English. He wanted Carlos to promise to come home when he graduated. Carlos promised, but in his heart he wasn't sure. He had not told his parents about Elinor, but he knew they had seen the letters arriving from America with her name on them. He was happy to get those letters and he answered them all.

One night a girl named Mercedes came to visit. Carlos' parents were glad to see her. They knew her parents well, and they knew that she and Carlos had been close friends when they were both in high school. They had always hoped that Carlos and Mercedes would get married someday, and her parents hoped so, too. Carlos and Mercedes sat down alone to have a talk. At first Carlos was uncomfortable. He talked about small, unimportant things like the weather. Mercedes asked him about his life in America. Again, he started to talk about unimportant things, but soon he was telling her about Elinor. It was impossible not to talk about her. Mercedes told him she knew he had met a girl. She could tell immediately by the way he acted toward her. She knew that might happen if he went to America, but at the same time, she was happy for him. She asked him what his plans were, but he wasn't sure. He only knew he had met a wonderful girl and he was happier than he had ever been in his life.

I. Using the following pictures, tell the story you have just read in your own words.

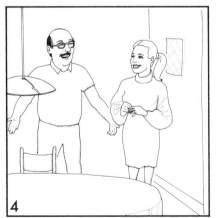

QUESTIONS FOR DISCUSSION

1. What words would you use to describe Carlos' father? Mercedes?

2. Do you feel sympathy for Carlos' father? Was Carlos right to promise as he did?

3. Do your parents have worries such as Carlos' father has? Do you have such worries?

4. Do you have a good friend like Mercedes? Can you tell the class about him or her?

II. Act out the story you have just read and heard. Choose students to take the parts of the persons in the story and improvise the dialogue. There are two scenes and three characters.

Scene 1   Setting: Carlos' house
    Characters: Carlos
         His Father
Scene 2   Setting: Carlos' house
    Characters: Carlos
         Mercedes

III. Write the dialogue for the scenes you have just acted out.

Quick Sketch

   a. Carlos' parents discussed their son's new American girlfriend. What did they say to each other? Improvise the scene between these two characters.

   b. Mercedes talked with one of her girlfriends about Carlos' new American girlfriend. What did the two girls say to each other? Improvise the scene between these two characters.

16 *CARLOS AND ELINOR* *IV*

When Carlos and Elinor returned to school in the fall, they started dating again. As before, they were together all the time. One night, several months after the school year had begun, Carlos called Elinor on the phone. He needed to be sure she was home because he wanted to come over and see her. He had something important to discuss with her.

Elinor thought she knew what Carlos wanted to talk about. She explained things to Sue, her roommate, and Sue agreed to go to the library and study so Carlos and Elinor could be alone. Soon after she left, Carlos came over. He told Elinor how he had come to feel about her. She talked about her feelings for him. He talked about his plans for the future. Then he asked Elinor to marry him. She didn't give him an answer that night. She needed time to think about it. But she didn't refuse.

I. Using the following pictures, tell the story you have just read in your own words.

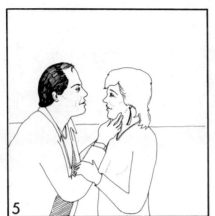

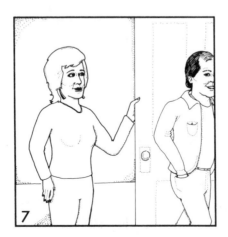

QUESTIONS FOR DISCUSSION

1. Should Carlos have proposed to Elinor at this time? Do you think he had enough time to consider it? Is he in a good position to marry?

2. Was Elinor right in asking Carlos to wait for an answer?

II. Act out the story you have just read and heard. Choose students to take the parts of the persons in the story and improvise the dialogue. There are two scenes and three characters.

Scene 1	Setting:	Carlos' room and Elinor's room (a phone conversation)
	Characters:	Carlos
		Elinor
Scene 2	Setting:	Elinor's room
	Characters:	Elinor
		Sue
		Carlos

III. Write the dialogue for the scenes you have just acted out.

EXTRA ACTIVITIES ———————————

Investigation

How do students at your school (students in general, not just international students) feel about marrying at this time of their lives? Talk to a group of students and report to the class.

CARLOS AND ELINOR   V

When he returned home after seeing Elinor, Carlos telephoned his parents. They were very upset. This was just what they had been afraid of. They didn't know the girl. They had always thought Carlos would marry Mercedes or some other girl from home. They asked him not to marry Elinor.

Elinor also telephoned her parents. They were unhappy, too. They wanted her to marry one day, but not until she finished her education. They wanted her to give herself more time and meet more men, men with a solid future. And they did not know anything about Carlos.

Carlos and Elinor did not know what to do. Carlos talked things over with Dave and Ernesto, a boy from his country. Ernesto thought Carlos should listen to his parents. They always knew best. And he thought marriage with a girl from another country would bring too many problems. But Dave felt that people should make their own decisions. Carlos was old enough to make an intelligent choice. And if two people loved each other, that was the important thing. Carlos listened to both of them. He was sure he still wanted to marry Elinor. But he worried.

I. Using the following pictures, retell the story you have just read in your own words.

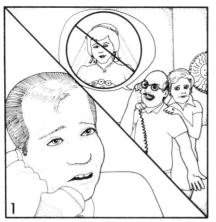

QUESTIONS FOR DISCUSSION

1. Whom do you feel more sympathetic toward, Carlos or his parents?

2. Are Elinor's parents right when they say she should finish her education?

3. Ernesto says parents know best. Do you think they always do?

4. Elinor's parents want her to marry a man with a future. Dave thinks love is the most important thing. Whom do you agree with more?

II. Act out the story you have just read and heard. Choose students to take the parts of the persons in the story and improvise the dialogue. There are three scenes and eight characters.

Scene 1	Setting:	Carlos' Room and His Parents' Home (a phone conversation)
	Characters:	Carlos
		His Mother and Father
Scene 2	Setting:	Elinor's Room and Her Parents' Home (a phone conversation)
	Characters:	Elinor
		Her Mother and Father
Scene 3	Setting:	Carlos' Room
	Characters:	Carlos
		Dave
		Ernesto

III. Write the dialogue for the scenes you have just acted out.

Investigation

How do international students in your school or community feel about marrying a person from the country where they are studying? How important is their parents' opinion in this matter? Do a study and report to the class.

18   *CARLOS AND ELINOR*   *VI*

Elinor talked things over with Sue. Sue suggested some things Elinor should think about—whether she loved Carlos enough to spend her life with him, whether she could live happily in Carlos' country or Carlos could live happily here, and, as Elinor's parents had wondered, whether Carlos had a promising future. Elinor thought seriously about all these things.

Then one night Elinor telephoned Carlos and asked him to come over. She had made her decision. Carlos came over immediately. He knocked on the door and Elinor let him in. They sat down on Elinor's couch and . . .

I. Using the following pictures, tell the story you have just read in your own words.

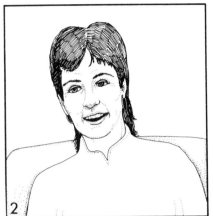

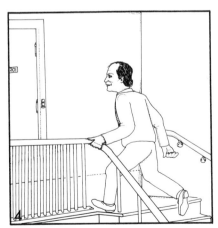

101

─── *QUESTIONS FOR DISCUSSION* ───

1. What words would you use to describe Sue?

2. Are the things Sue told Elinor to think about important?

3. Are there other important things Sue didn't mention?

4. Do you think you could live happily outside of your own country? Could a foreign spouse live happily with you in your country?

II. Act out the story you have just read and heard. Choose students to take the parts of the persons in the story and improvise the dialogue. You will have to decide how the story ends. There are two scenes and three characters.

Scene 1	Setting:	Elinor's Room
	Characters:	Elinor
		Sue
Scene 2	Setting:	Elinor's Room
	Characters:	Elinor
		Sue
		Carlos

III. Write the dialogue for the scenes you have just acted out.

Quick Sketch

After you have decided how the story ends, you can improvise the following scenes:

a. Elinor tells her roommate about her decision and they discuss it.

b. Elinor phones her parents and informs them of her decision and her parents react.

c. Carlos tells Dave about Elinor's decision and they discuss it.

d. Carlos phones his parents and informs them of Elinor's decision and they react.

19 THE LAST STORY

Somewhere in this class there is a student, and probably more than one, who has an interesting story to tell. That story could be written down and acted out. It might be a story from childhood or a more recent experience at home or in a foreign country. It might be a happy story or a sad one. But someone in the class has a story that the class could write and act out. Maybe the entire class could do one story, with one group doing the writing, another group making the pictures, another group acting it out, and a fourth group writing the dialogue. Or perhaps the class could work on several stories at one time. In that case, one member of each group could do each task, such as making the pictures. After the stories have been presented, the class could vote to choose the best story or the best presentation. Or the groups could exchange. One group could take another group's story and act it out.

You've been telling someone else's stories until now. Now it is time to tell your own. And that will probably be the best story of all.